GAZING IN WONDER

**Developing
spirituality
with young
children**

Jill Fuller

**Illustrated by
Liz McIntosh**

Kevin
Mayhew

First published in 1996 by
KEVIN MAYHEW LTD
Buxhall
Stowmarket
Suffolk IP14 3DJ

© 1996 Kevin Mayhew Ltd

1 2 3 4 5 6 7 8 9

ISBN 0 86209 767 3
Catalogue No 1500041

Front cover illustration by Rob Payne

Edited by Peter Dainty and Stephen Haddelsey
Cover design by Jonathan Stroulger
Typesetting by Louise Selfe
Printed and bound in Great Britain

CONTENTS

INTRODUCTION

The aim of this series of books – *Gazing in Wonder, Looking Beyond* and *Dreams and Visions* – is to help and support those concerned with the spiritual development of children. The hope is to foster a pattern of spirituality which will continue to be a source of refreshment and renewal into adulthood.

Many of us are indebted to those in our own lives who launched us on our spiritual pilgrimage. It may have been a parent, a teacher, a peer at school or college, a priest or lay person who encouraged us on our first steps. The influences we each experienced on our own journey may be many and varied, but for me one of the greatest privileges has been to share my journey with children. Without fail, whether they knew it or not, they have helped me to recognise what is really significant in the pattern of my life and have always faced me with the hard questions which as adults we can become so adept at avoiding.

This book does not therefore presume to mark out a spiritual path for children, for I believe that children's honesty and openness to events is closer to the heart of spirituality than anything I can offer. Rather, the following ideas are intended for anyone willing to be a companion and partner to children, encouraging and affirming their steps on their unique and individual spiritual pilgrimage.

The decision to be a partner on this pilgrimage will be a risky one. It will mean a commitment of our time and attention. It will require humility in realising that children have much to teach us; the wonder of a small child seeing snow for the first time can re-awaken our sense of the miraculous;

the insatiable curiosity of an eight year old intent on finding out how something works can nudge us out of our complacent indifference; the heart-searching questioning of a young adult trying to find a purpose and significance for their own life can open us again to consider the ambiguities and suffering in our own lives. Without doubt the honest sharing of any pilgrimage, whether it be a simple journey, a lifelong relationship or a venture into spirituality, will expose us to that vulnerability which so often precedes real change and growth. Change and growth can be painful as well as stimulating and before we set out on this partnership perhaps we need as parents, priests or educators to ask ourselves what we want for our children in the area of spiritual development.

ATTENDING, REFLECTING AND CONNECTING

The spiritual life is an act of committed risk. It means that we cease to listen to the endless chatter of the world around, in order to attend to stillness and understand that world more fully. It requires that we set aside the urgency of the immediate task in order to reflect, and it demands that we make connections between what we perceive in the stillness and what we know to be happening around us.

Attending

Attending is the pre-requisite to any learning or development. Attending requires both stillness and silence. Yet many children are unable to be still in body or quiet in mind. The mores of the time associate speed and noise with success. Fast cars, a full Filofax, the constant murmur of radio, television or computer games means that the chance to experience silence or to be really still is denied many children. Before any spirituality can begin, we have to reaffirm that both stillness and silence are 'alright' and to rediscover the skills of listening attentively.

Attending does not only involve listening but also directing our whole being towards a single focus. 'Be still and know that I am God,' writes the Psalmist. To 'be still', to fully attend, we need to be able to relax whilst remaining alert. It involves our breathing, our body posture, the direction of our imagination and will. The practice of attending, that is of listening and of being still, allows us to be totally present in the 'now' of this moment.

Reflecting

A journey of spiritual development should provide opportunities for reflection: time to contemplate at more leisure the wonder of the created world, to turn over in our minds issues of justice and morality, to examine the behaviour of ourselves as well as others and to look with compassion upon our communities near and far. Opportunities should be given to reflect upon feelings, negative as well as positive, relationships with others: moments beyond the ordinary and everyday. There should be time to think about our values and attitudes and to recognise our prejudices. We should seek to encourage our children to ask the ultimate questions and to look without fear at the hard issues, as well as to celebrate the joys, of our everyday lives.

Connecting

It seems to me that a spiritual life is both arid and meaningless if it does not have

a direct effect upon our daily lives. What we make of the attending and reflecting must be of a piece and have an integrity which we can own for ourselves and see mirrored in our life-styles. It must be an honest reflection of our individual natures and it must be true to the experiences of life. A path of spiritual development which concentrates only on the happy, the creative, the socially acceptable side of our personalities and society cannot be 'in spirit and in truth'. We must look at our fears as well as celebrate our courage, acknowledge our anger and brokenness as well as rejoice when we feel whole and at peace.

The children we travel with on their spiritual pilgrimage are the same ones who see the doubts, fears and repercussions of child murders and watch the television news as it reports atrocities around the world. It will not suffice to give them a spiritual diet of the Peter Pan variety. The philosophy of 'Clap your hands and Tinkerbell won't die' can only have a passing part in the development of a mature person. Likewise we cannot reflect on the created world as a focus for wonder and worship if we are not prepared to look critically at our responsibilities to the whole eco-structure and the way these responsibilities must alter our lifestyle.

Encouraging children on the road of spiritual development will be no doddle. If taken seriously it may lead us to both peace and fulfilment, but our journey may include the dark night of the soul.

The suggestions offered in this, the first book of the series, seek to follow the young child's natural spirituality. The ideas have been collected through years of working with children both as a teacher in schools and as a voluntary worker with children in churches, and through the time of parenting my own children.

They have been collected by a process of osmosis, absorbed as I experienced and delighted in the privilege of living and working alongside adults and children who were themselves on a pilgrimage of prayer and spirituality.

USING THIS BOOK

There are seven main sections:

EXPLORING
THANKSGIVING
ATTENTIVE LISTENING
WORSHIP AND WONDER
THINKING OF OTHERS
TRUSTING
IMAGINING

I have named these sections 'Prayer Moods'. The mood is meant to indicate the general atmosphere or feeling of the prayer. Each Prayer Mood has one or more accompanying 'Prayer Focus' pages. The Prayer Focus is an idea to help the child to enter into the spirit of the prayer mood. For each theme a 'Focus Page' has been provided which can be photocopied for the children to use individually, in group work or to take home. The purpose of the Focus Page is to encourage the skills of Attending, Reflecting and Connecting. Although some of the ideas on the Focus Pages involve activity, this is not meant to be undertaken busily or as a compulsory duty. Many of the ideas can be developed gradually, perhaps over several days or weeks. Sometimes the children's own direction may replace those on the Focus Page. At all times the prayer companion or teacher should be sensitive to the promptings of the children, choosing and adapting the material to suit the particular needs of their group.

Spiritual development means different things to different people. The following pages inevitably reflect my own beliefs, background and experience, but I hope they will be of use to all those who seek to travel alongside children in their spiritual quest.

JILL FULLER

ACKNOWLEDGEMENTS

The publishers wish to express their gratitude to the following for permission to include copyright material in this book:

Campbell Connelly & Co Ltd, 8/9 Frith Street, London W1V 5TZ for *He gave me eyes so I could see* © Copyright 1970 Hye-Fye Music Ltd. Used by permission. All rights reserved

Mrs Hazel A. Charlton for *In the morning early (I listen and I listen)*.
Jubilate Hymns, 61 Chessel Avenue, Southampton SO19 4DY for *Can you be sure* © Copyright Geoffrey Marshall Taylor/Julibate Hymns.

Kingsway's Thankyou Music, PO Box 75, Eastbourne, East Sussex BN23 6NW for *Thank you Lord, for this fine day* © Copyright 1971 Celebration/Kingsway's Thankyou Music, Europe & Commonwealth (exc. Canada, Australasia & Africa).

Stainer and Bell Ltd, PO Box 110, Victoria House, 23 Gruneisen Road, Finchley, London N3 1DZ for *Jesus' hands were kind hands*.

A *Rainbow Song* and *Springtime* © 1996 Kevin Mayhew Ltd, Rattlesden, Suffolk IP30 0SZ. Words by Michael Forster.

First Prayer Mood
EXPLORING

Yet it was you who took me from the womb; you kept me safe on my mother's breasts. Psalm 22:9

The focus of this prayer time is to help the children to explore God's gifts of body and mind and to foster the awareness of God as a loving creator who wants us to enjoy his world.

Each prayer time in this first Prayer Mood will focus on enjoying a different sense of the body: sight, hearing, speaking, thinking and imagining, touching, moving.

The words of the following poem have been used as a framework for the ideas in this section.

> He gave me eyes so I could see
> the wonders of the world;
> without my eyes I could not see
> the other boys and girls.
> He gave me ears so I could hear
> the wind and rain and sea.
> I've got to tell it to the world,
> He made me.
>
> He gave me lips so I could speak
> and say what's in my mind;
> without my lips I could not speak
> a single word or line.
> He made my mind so I could think,
> and choose what I should be.
> I've got to tell it to the world,
> He made me.
>
> He gave me hands so I could touch,
> and hold a thousand things;
> I need my hands to help me write,
> to help me fetch and bring.
> These feet he made so I could run,
> He meant me to be free.
> I've got to tell it to the world,
> He made me.

(From *Come and Praise* BBC Publications.)

Prayer Focus 1

What do you see?

Read the children the first four lines of this poem:

He gave me eyes so I could see
the wonders of the world;
without my eyes I could not see
the other boys and girls.

(from *Come & Praise,* BBC Publications)

Share with the children what they love seeing:

– a cobweb covered in raindrops?
– oil on a puddle?
– a shiny conker?
– the silhouette of chimney pots and roofs against the sky?

Choose one object for a focus and spend time helping the children to describe what they see and encouraging their observations.

Allow the children time to draw or paint what they are enjoying seeing.

Using the children's words, write underneath their picture their description and observations.

Be sure to affirm their work by putting it where it can be seen.

Ending Prayer

Thank you, God, for our eyes.
Thank you for the gift of sight.
Thank you for all the shades of colour we can see.
Thank you for all the different shapes we can see.
Thank you that we can see the tiny details of things we hold close to us.
Thank you that we can see far into the distance.
Thank you that we can see all the wonders of your world. Amen.

What do you see?

Joanna is looking at a cobweb on her garden fence.
She is looking at the pattern of the web.
She likes to watch the sunshine reflecting
    from the raindrops on the web.
What do you like looking at?

Different views

Choose an object to look at with the children. This could be a stone, a fir cone, a photograph from a newspaper, a reproduction of a picture. Look at the object together and share with the children what they each observe. Allow time for each child to express what they see. Share the things which you have noticed.

Talk about how each individual sees things slightly differently and in their own special way.

Look at some things under a magnifying glass. How does seeing things close-up change what we can observe?

Find somewhere with a view into the distance. How far can we see? What happens when we move nearer?

Develop the idea that a loving God has made each one of us unique and with a special view of the world to share with others.

Ending Prayer

Thank you, God, for all the variety of people in your world.
Thank you that we each have a special view which only we can see.
Help us to share our special view with others.
Help us to listen to what others can tell us about your world. Amen.

Different views

Joanna and Sam are on the top of a hill.
They are looking all around them.
Joanna notices a farmer working on a tractor in the
    nearby fields.
Sam finds a snail shell at his feet and looks at the
    colours in it.
What do you notice in this picture?

PRAYER FOCUS 3

Changing views

Make an opportunity to look at some objects several times but in different seasons, e.g. a tree.

In the autumn help the children to watch for changes in the colour of the tree and to observe what happens. (Remember that everybody experiences a first autumn.) How do they feel as they watch the leaves fall? Perhaps the children may like to press some of the leaves and make a picture? Compare the leaves and the fruits of different trees.

Visit the same tree in the winter. What can the children see now which was hidden before? Does the tree show a new beauty? Search for signs that the tree is still alive.

Visit the same tree as spring approaches. Help the children to observe what is happening. Make sure they can see the buds on the tree. If possible, carefully cut a small twig and put it in water indoors to observe the opening of the leaves. Outside notice in which order the trees show their leaves.

In the summer enjoy the shade, the dappled light, the birds and animals living in the tree.

Help the children to think about the cycle of change, times when the tree seemed alive, times when the tree seemed dead but was still alive, the new life of the tree, their feelings when watching the different changes in the tree.

Ending Prayer

Thank you, God, for all the changes we
   can see around us:
   for the warmth of summer when the
   days are long and so much is growing;
   for the autumn when the days grow
   shorter and we watch the changes in the
   world around us;
   for the winter when the trees and plants
   seem to disappear;
   for the promise of the new life of spring.
Help us to know that you are with us
   through all the changes in our life.

   Amen.

Changing views

These are pictures of a horse chestnut tree in
  spring, summer, autumn and winter.
What do you notice about the tree?
How has it changed?
Is there any season of the tree's life which you
  like best?
Can you find something which you enjoy about
  every season?
Do you think every season is important for the tree?

PRAYER FOCUS 4

In the dark

With the children explore what it would mean to be unable to see.

With their eyes shut can they:
 – remember what is in the room?
 – remember what the adult is wearing?
 – put on their socks?

Talk about what the darkness means to them. What do they like about the night? How does the darkness change their perception of shape, colour, objects?

Talk about how God made the day and the night, the sun, the moon and the stars and is present in all of Creation.

Ending Prayer

Thank you, God, for the day and the night;
   for the wonder of each dawn and the
   return of the warmth and light of the sun.
Thank you that the light helps us to see.
Thank you for the night time when the
   world seems to rest;
   for the wonders of the moon, the stars and
   planets and the beauty of the night sky.
Help us to remember you created both
   darkness and light.
Help us to feel you close to us when it is
   light *and* when we experience darkness.
   Amen.

In the dark

These two pictures show the view from Sam's
  window in the daytime and at night.
What are the differences?
What do you like about the view in the daytime?
Is there anything you don't like?
What do you like about the view at night?
Is there anything you don't like?

Using our ears

He gave me ears so I could hear the wind and rain and sea.
(from *Come and Praise*, BBC Publications)

A. What can you hear?

Choose a quiet place and allow the children a minute to listen and note the sounds they hear.

Concentrate first on far away sounds outside the room: traffic, people passing, birdsong, work people.

Concentrate on nearer sounds within the room: a kettle boiling, someone moving, the water moving in the radiators.

Concentrate on sounds our bodies make: breathing, sniffing, tummy rumbling.

Talk about how it feels to listen so attentively. Were there noises they did not usually hear? What did they think about when they heard the sounds?

B. Different sounds

Choose a variety of things which might make a sound, e.g. a drum, two spoons, water to pour into a glass, a comb, tissue paper. Use each item to make a sound. With the children, talk about how each sound is different.

On another occasion have the items ready behind a screen. Take it in turns to make a noise and guess which item is being used to make the noise.

Talk about how each thing has its own unique sound. (You would be surprised if you heard a sound like that of stones rattling when water was poured.)

Find a CD or tape featuring different instruments (a piano concerto, a violin sonata, a cello, a trumpet voluntary). Establish which instrument the children like best, and why.

Ending Prayer

Thank you, God, for all the many sounds
we can hear:
>   the clatter of pots and pans;
>   the whirr and bang of machinery;
>   the sound of the wind in the trees;
>   the sound of the rain on the window;
>   the shout of a crowd at a football match;
>   the voice of a friend;
>   the purr of a cat.
In the silence now we thank you for our
>   favourite sound . . . Amen.

Using our ears

Joanna is listening carefully.
What sounds did she hear?
What did you hear when *you* were listening?

Silence and sound

A. A quiet time

With the children, take time each day to sit together for a moment (start with half a minute) and to enjoy complete silence without music, radio or television. Make sure this is presented as a time of positive joint restfulness and pleasure, never as a punishment or a way of silencing the children. It could be while a drink was being shared. Share your thoughts after the silence. Assure the children that it is safe and acceptable to be silent and still. Discuss with the children a place where they could be still and silent. Gradually increase the time-span, but be sensitive to the needs and mood of the children. Compulsion would be a mistake.

Make sure that the children are comfortable. A carpeted area or cushions would help, and space to be away from the distractions of others around them.

Ending Prayer

Thank you, God, for stillness.
Thank you, God, for quiet.
Thank you, God, for silence. Amen.

B. Listen to this

Clap a simple rhythm and ask the children to echo the same rhythm back. How accurate were they?

Tell a simple story (see example in the Appendix on page 80) or read a simple poem, or listen to a story on tape. How much can each member of the group remember? How attentively were they listening?

With the children talk about times when there is a lot of noise around us. Do we have to choose what we will listen to? How do they make sure they can hear what they need to hear?

How much do we use God's gift of hearing to really listen?

Ending Prayer

Lord Jesus, there are many sounds around us:
    loud sounds which take up our attention;
    quiet sounds which only whisper.
Help us to choose how we listen.
Help us to listen with care. Amen.

Favourite sounds

Sam likes the sound of the waves crashing against the
  sea shore.
Joanna enjoys the sound of a trumpet playing.
Can you draw your favourite sound?

PRAYER FOCUS 7

What can you say?

*He gave me lips so I could speak
and say what's in my mind.
Without my lips I could not speak
a single word or line.*
(from *Come and Praise,* BBC Publications)

Encourage the children to experiment to discover how many different sounds they can make with their lips and tongue.

They may like to watch their lips and mouth in a mirror while they make the sounds – bbb, brrr, ccc, ddd, pppp, shhh.

Try clicking noises, dripping noises, clopping noises, kissing noises.

Can they make a noise which sounds like: the swishing of the sea, the hooves of a horse, the rustling of leaves, an aeroplane, a car screeching, rain falling on a metal dustbin?

Collect some words which have a similar sound and enjoy saying them – swishing, swirling, swaying, sweeping, swelling, swamping, swerving, swinging, swivelling, swiping.

Try making up some tongue twisters:

Penelope Perkins painted pretty pictures peacefully perched on a parrot.

Thomas thankfully tipped his tickling turtle into the tank.

Ending Prayer

Thank you, God, for the fun of making
different sounds.
Thank you for words which can explain
how we feel.
Thank you for words which make us laugh.
Thank you for words to comfort and
encourage each other.
Thank you for the gift of speech. Amen.

What can you say?

Here are some tongue twisters to take home to try with the family:

Betty bought a beautiful blue bonnet.

Betty bought a beautiful blue bonnet before buying bunches of black bananas.

Tiny Thomas tried to turn the tank.

Tiny Thomas tried to turn the tank towards the tomato.

Happy Harry helped his hippopotamus hurry home.

Samuel sells sandwiches on sunny Saturdays.

Theo thanked Thomas for thoughtfully throwing thistles.

Here is a tongue twister for you to colour in:

Charlie the chimpanzee chewed his chair cheerfully.

Make up a tongue twister of your own and draw a picture to illustrate it.

Different voices

Encourage the children to realise the wide range of different voices they can adopt. Can they speak quietly, loudly, shout? When might they need to use their different voices? Can they make their voice sound gentle, encouraging, reassuring, cross, complaining? When might they need to use these voices?

How low or high can they sing?
What kind of voice would they use
  – to comfort a frightened animal?
  – to warn a friend of danger?
  – to share a secret?
  – when visiting someone who is feeling ill?
  – to call for help?

Ending Prayer

Thank you, God, for all the ways we can use our voices –
  for gentle voices to comfort those who are sad;
  for strong voices to sing when we are happy;
  for loud voices to shout when we are in danger.
Help us to choose the right voice. Amen.

Different voices

Look at these pictures.
What do you think Sam is saying?
What kind of voice would he use?

PRAYER FOCUS 9

Saying what's in our mind

With the children, talk about how speech is a gift from God to help us to communicate and understand each other. Discuss how we sometimes 'speak' with our bodies.

With the children, collect some pictures of people. Try to find as many different moods, expressions and situations as possible.

Talk about what the people in the picture are doing and how they are feeling. Help them to recognise sadness, excitement, anger, boredom, fear, and to discuss their feelings. Help them to mime their happy, sad, angry or frightened faces. Ask the children to wave goodbye, beckon someone to come closer, put a finger on their lips to ask for silence.

Talk about how God wants us to share how we feel and is interested in our lives.

Ending Prayer

Thank you, God, for all the ways we can
show how we are feeling –
by our words;
by our voices;
by the way we sit or walk or move.
Help us to notice how other people are
feeling.
Help us to recognise when they are tired,
sad, excited, happy or frightened.
Thank you that we can always tell you
what is on our minds and how we are
feeling.
Help us to understand that whatever we
are feeling you always love us. Amen.

Saying what's in our mind

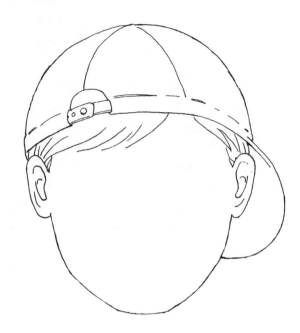

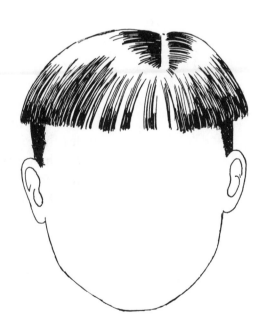

On these faces draw a face which is happy, sad,
frightened or angry.

Pictures in our minds

He made my mind so I could think
and choose what I could be.
(From *Come and Praise*, BBC Publications)

Ask the children to close their eyes and imagine what you describe. Make the first 'picture' easy and based on familiar things. Gradually build up to more complicated 'pictures' including walks, events in the past, anticipated events of the future, an imaginary walk or event. Encourage the children to tell you what they can 'see'.

Can they imagine
  – their teddy bear?
  – the clothes they are wearing today?
  – the room they are in now?
  – where they sit for breakfast?
  – their bedroom?
  – a walk by the sea?
  – a visit to the fair?
  – what they would like to do tomorrow?
  – a picture they would like to paint?

Talk about those pictures in their minds which are based on memories, and those which result from imagining things which might happen in the future.

Talk about stories which are 'made up' and the excitement of creating or inventing something new.

Ending Prayer

Thank you, God, for our minds –
  for the the fun of thinking, inventing and new ideas;
  for the excitement of planning;
  for the wonder of our imagination;
  for the joy of creating;
  for the pleasure of remembering. Amen.

Pictures in our minds

Look at this picture carefully.
Now turn the picture over, close your eyes and see
   what you can remember.
You may like to colour the picture in.

Looking at our hands

He gave me hands so I could touch
and hold a thousand things.
I need my hands to help me write,
to help me fetch and bring.
(From *Come and Praise,* BBC Publications)

Spend time with the children looking at your hands together. Compare the sizes, the length of each finger, the feel of the skin, where the fingers bend, the lines and finger prints. Experiment to find out which finger is easier to bend on its own, which fingers we use most to point, to pick up things, to tie laces.

Compare what you can do with the right and left hand. Experiment with the children closing their eyes to see if you can touch a hand without the person knowing.

You may like the children to draw around the hand, make paint hand prints or a finger painting.

Ending Prayer

Thank you, God, for the wonder of our
   hands –
   for the patterns of lines on the palms and
   fingertips;
   for our knuckles and wrists and the way
   our hands can stretch and curl;
   for the sensitivity of our fingertips and the
   gift of touch;
   for hands which are gentle;
   for hands which are strong. Amen.

Looking at our hands

Here are the outlines of the back and palm of a hand.
Draw in the nails the knuckles and other marks.
Draw in the lines you can see on the palms of your
  hands and on your fingertips.

PRAYER FOCUS 12

A different feel

With the children collect items with different textures. Try to include as many textures as possible – rough, smooth, cold, warm, furry, silky, scratchy, sticky, spongy.

Give the children plenty of experience in handling the textures and discussing what they like feeling. Which textures do they like or dislike?

Can they imagine the feel of
- clean sheets?
- sand between their toes?
- cold ice cream on their tongue?
- sticky jam around their mouth?
- a boot full of water?

Are some textures more suitable for different occasions? Would they like a furry plate for their dinner, rough sheets for their bed?

Play a game with a 'magic bag'. In the bag put a number of items which have different shapes and textures: a pot scourer, a cone, a packet of jelly, a furry toy, a sponge, a metal key, a marble, etc. Let the children take turns to put their hand into the bag and feel the items one by one, describing what they feel and guessing what the item is. They may like to draw what they can feel in the bag on the Focus Page.

Ending Prayer

Thank you, God, for all the different
    textures we can touch –
    the roughness of the playground;
    the smoothness of a cat's fur;
    the stickiness of jam;
    water running through our fingers;
    the coldness of snow;
    the hardness of a pebble.
Thank you for the variety of all that there
    is to feel and touch. Amen.

A different feel

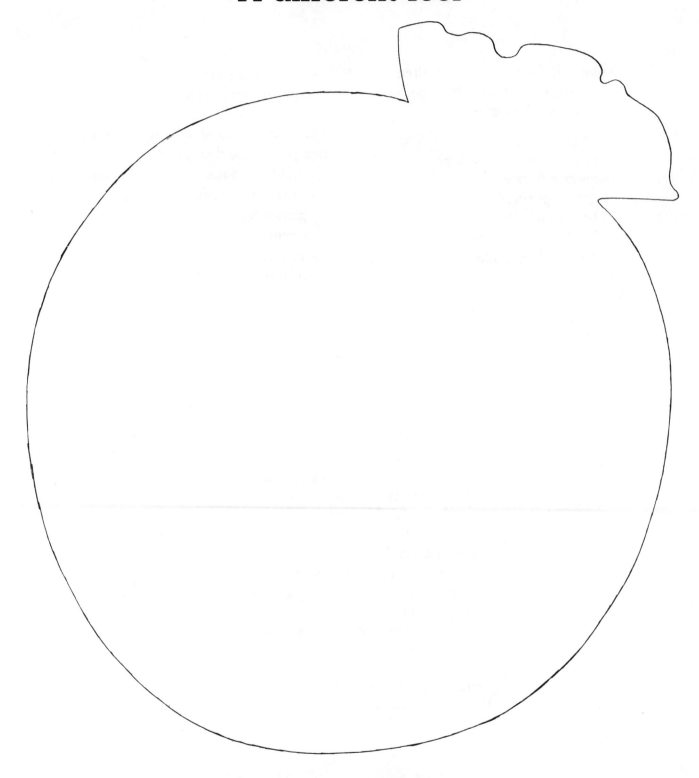

What can you feel in the bag?
In this bag draw what you have felt.
Afterwards compare it with what was in the bag.

We need our hands

Explore all the things the children can do with their hands. Give the opportunity for plenty of experiment.

Can they
- thread beads on a string?
- fasten a buckle?
- draw a picture?
- lay the table?
- build a tower of bricks?
- pour milk on cereal?

Try to do some things with one hand.
Can they
- put on a sock?
- clean their teeth?
- spread butter on toast?

With the children talk about all the ways people use their hands:
- building houses
- driving machines
- gardening
- typing
- writing
- painting
- sewing
- playing an instrument
- as a surgeon or doctor

Ending Prayer

Thank you, God, that we can do so many
   things with our hands –
   for the useful things we can do –
   laying the table for dinner, dressing
   ourselves, eating our food,
   for the kind things we can do –
   helping to carry, comforting a friend,
   stroking our pet;
   for the creative things we can do –
   playing an instrument, gardening,
   painting.
Help us to use our hands well. Amen.

32

We need our hands

Look at these pictures.
What are the people doing with their hands?
What do you like doing with your hands?
Draw what you like doing in the space.

PRAYER FOCUS 14

Helping hands

Ask the children to do something which involves their hands:
- please could you pick up my pencil?
- could you pour me a glass of water?

With the children think of all the things they can do to help others with their hands.

Can they think of times they have seen, either in their own lives or on television, others use their hands unkindly, to hit or to cause pain.

Discuss how hands can either bring comfort or pain, can help or hinder.

You could tell the story of Jesus healing the leper (Mark 1:40-44). How would the leper have felt when Jesus touched him?

Encourage them to do something this week to help someone else with the hands God has given them.

Let the children sing 'Jesus' hands were kind hands' (see Appendix B).

Ending Prayer

We give thanks for the gift of our hands.
   May we use them today to help others:
to share love with the lonely,
to comfort the wounded and the sick,
to carry the burden for those who are
sick or tired.

   Amen.

Helping hands

Look at these pictures.
How are the people using their hands to help others?
In the space draw something you can do with your
hands to help others.

Using our feet

These feet he made so I can run,
He meant me to be free.
(From *Come and Praise,* BBC Publications)

Let the children look carefully at their feet. Ask them to look at the length of their toes; where the foot bends; the shape of the instep; the ankle joint. Let them draw round their feet.

Let them discover what their feet can do – by picking up a hanky with their toes; drawing a picture with their toes; bending their toes separately; controlling a ball with their feet; walking on tip-toe; walking on their heels; walking very quietly; stamping, shuffling or skipping; varying the speed of their walking; walking tall; walking bent over.

Then help the children to celebrate their feet by devising a simple dance-movement to show what they can do with their feet. Try to include steps in different directions, short and long steps, slow and fast steps, skips, jumps and sliding steps.

Ending Prayer

Thank you, God, for our feet and for freedom of movement –
> for the fun of running and jumping;
> for the joy of skipping and dancing;
> for times when we take long strides
> and times when we take tiny steps;
> for walking quickly when our journey is urgent;
> for walking slowly when we have time to dream;
> for times when our feet follow busy streets;
> for times when our feet wander over open paths.
Help us to know that you are travelling with us wherever we walk. Amen.

Using our feet

Here are some pictures of children doing different
  things with their feet.
Imagine that you are doing them.
What does it feel like?
Which one do you like doing best?
Draw a picture of what you like doing with your bare
  feet.

Second Prayer Mood
THANKSGIVING

I have set my (rain)bow in the clouds, and it shall be a sign of the covenant between me and the earth. Genesis 9:13

The focus of this prayer time is to foster a sense of thanksgiving for the beauty of creation, both for the world around us and for God's love.

Thanksgiving for God's loving care

Remind the children of the story of Noah and God's promise. With the children talk about how we can see God's love in the world around us: the beauty of a sunset, the fun of playing with water, the delicious fruits and vegetables we enjoy.

Let them sing this 'Rainbow Song' – a thanksgiving for God's faithfulness. (To the tune of *An English Country Garden* – see Appendix B.)

Red, orange, yellow turning to green,
can you see the rainbow gleaming?
Violet and purple, ending in blue,
through the rain,
God's smile is beaming!

Hope is shining all around,
reaching down to touch the ground,
shining in the sky above us,
in the saddest of days
in many kinds of ways,
God reminds us how he loves us.

Ending Prayer

We give thanks for God's promise
of unending love and hope.
May we feel God's strength and care
near us every day.
May we recognise God's love in everything
we see of beauty and kindness.

Amen.

Thanksgiving for God's loving care

The rainbow is a sign of God's promise.
He promised that 'as long as the earth endures, seed
time and harvest, cold and heat, summer and winter,
day and night shall not cease.' Genesis 8:22
Here are four pictures to remind us of God's promise.
Colour them in.

Thanksgiving for the beauty of the earth

Make a Rainbow Shaker: Have ready one length of ribbon, wool or crêpe paper for every colour of the rainbow (red, orange, yellow, green, blue, indigo, violet). These lengths can either be sellotaped securely to a small piece of dowelling or attached to a piece of card.

Safety Note: If using dowelling make sure there are no sharp ends which could catch a child's eye.

Help the children to link each colour to a different aspect of God's creation, e.g. green with all plants and trees.

Teach the children the chorus of the hymn 'Thank you, Lord' (*Come and Praise*, BBC Publications).

Thank you, Lord, for this new day,
Thank you, Lord, for this new day,
Thank you, Lord, for this new day,
Right where we are.

Chorus:
Alleluia, praise the Lord,
Alleluia, praise the Lord,
Alleluia, praise the Lord,
Right where we are.

Everyone sings the 'Thank you' hymn passing the 'rainbow shaker' around the circle. At the end of the chorus, the child holding the shaker chooses a colour and thanks God for something of that colour in creation which they enjoy, e.g.

'Thank you, God, for the blue of the sky.'
'Thank you, God, for the purple of heather.'
'Thank you, God, for the orange of the sun.'
'Thank you, God, for the red of fire.'

Ending Prayer

Thank you, God, for the gift of all the colours of the rainbow which we can see in the world around us. Amen.

Thanksgiving for the beauty of the earth

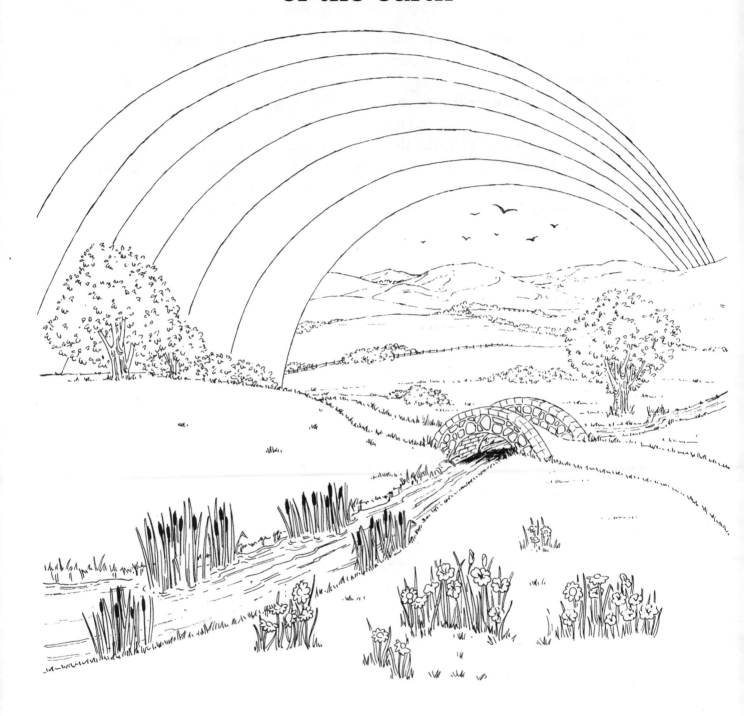

Do you know all the colours of the rainbow?
They are red, orange, yellow, green, blue, indigo and
  violet.
Can you colour in this rainbow?

Thanksgiving for God's colourful world

Make a 'Rainbow Exhibition'. Ask the children to choose one of the colours from the rainbow and to think of all the things they enjoy which are that colour, e.g. red . . . thanksgiving for fire and its warmth, certain flowers and leaves, the red breast of a robin, tomatoes, certain apples, peppers, radishes, the berries on a holly tree, strawberries and raspberries.

With the children, make a colour exhibition with the theme of one colour. For red this could include a model fire engine, a red ball, a red ribbon, a red candle etc.

Give time for the children to talk about their contribution to the exhibition. What do they like about that colour?

At the end give thanks for the colour.

Ending Prayer

Thank you, God, for the colour (red).

Amen.

(You could then ask each child to give thanks for the red item they have brought to the exhibition.)

Thanksgiving for God's colourful world

Look at this picture.

Can you find some holly berries, a post box, a postman's van, a robin?

What colour will you use to colour them?

When you have coloured them, colour the whole picture.

Third Prayer Mood
ATTENTIVE LISTENING

Hear and give ear; do not be haughty, for the Lord has spoken. Jeremiah 13:15.

The focus of this prayer time is to encourage attentive listening and to experience being listened to and listening to each other.

PRAYER FOCUS 19

We can hear what you're saying
A. The listening shell

You will need a simple shell, or a stone if a shell is not available. It should be a comfortable size to hold. The rule is that only the person holding the shell is allowed to speak and will not be interrupted for one to two minutes. The shell is passed from child to child and everyone has an opportunity to speak about anything they wish. It could be something they enjoyed during the day or something which is worrying them. At the end of the time the other children may make one comment or question which, hopefully, will show they have attended carefully, e.g. 'I'm glad you had a good time at the party.' 'It's sad when your friends won't let you join in the game they're playing.'

B. The listening artist

Provide the children with plain paper and coloured crayons. Explain that this is a game to see how carefully they can listen. You would like them to draw what you describe.

Give simple examples first:
   – draw a blue circle
   – draw a face with a smiling mouth
   – draw a house with two windows and one door
   – draw a red ball

Look at their pictures. Have they listened to what was described?

Explain that they are going to play at being a 'listening artist'. They are going to draw a picture which you describe. They will not see the picture but simply draw what you say is in it.

Sit the children facing away from you. Describe the pictures on the Focus Page slowly, one at a time. 'The listening artists' draw what they hear. Finally, compare their pictures with the ones on the Focus Page. How carefully did the artists listen? How accurate is their picture?

Ending Prayer

Help us to listen to each other, Lord. Amen.

48

We can hear what you're saying

Describe these pictures to the children for the
'Listening Artist' game.

We know how to listen

A. A listening game

One person is the instructor and the other the listener. The instructor gives simple commands and the listener sees how accurately he/she can follow the commands. The commands can gradually become more complex:

– pick up your teddy
– pick up your teddy and put her on a chair
– pick up your teddy and put her on the chair by the table
– pick up your teddy, dress her in a red coat and put her on the chair
– pick up your teddy, dress her in a red coat and walk her around the room, showing her two things

Ending Prayer

Lord Jesus, help us to use all of our minds when we listen. Amen.

B. A listening song

Teach the children the song 'I listen and I listen' (*Come and Praise,* BBC Publications).
The children can learn the final lines: 'I listen and I listen'.

In the morning early
I go down to the sea
and see the mist on the shore;
I listen, and I listen.

When I go to the rocks
I go looking for shells
and feel the sand beneath my feet;
I listen, and I listen.

When the stormy day comes
Waves crash on the cliffs
and the wind whistles through my hair;
I listen, and I listen.

And at night when I sleep
and the sea is calm
the gentle waves lap the shore;
I listen and I listen

I sometimes think that God
is talking to me
when I hear the sound of the sea;
I listen, and I listen.
I listen, and I listen.

Discuss how God is in all things and how all sounds can be a way of listening to him.

Ending Prayer

Lord Jesus, help us to listen to all the sounds around us and to know that you are near. Amen.

We know how to listen

Look at these pictures.
Which picture do you think best matches the words in each verse of the song?

Fourth Prayer Mood
WORSHIP AND WONDER

O Lord, our sovereign, how majestic is your name in all the earth. Psalm 8:1

The focus of the prayer time is to foster in the children a sense of wonder at the world around them and to recognise miracles in the everyday.

PRAYER FOCUS 21

A miracle tray

The children will need a table in the prayer area, where their 'miracles' can be displayed. If that is difficult, an individual tray or shoe box, which they can keep in the prayer area, might be possible. On this tray can be put 'treasures' which they collect and enjoy looking at. It could be a feather, a collection of seeds, a leaf, a picture of an animal or bird, a photograph of mountains or the sea. The idea is to add to the tray gradually and to spend time pondering the miracle of each item during the prayer time, bringing to mind the creativity and strength of God. Take time to allow each child to describe their treasure carefully.

Arrange the children's 'miracles' carefully on the tray or table. Affirm their observations and accept what they notice as being a 'miracle'.

Ending Prayer

(Help each child to offer their treasure as an act of thanksgiving. Use a simple sentence which each child can adapt. Encourage each child to define what quality of their 'miracle' they especially want to give thanks for.)

We worship you, creator God, for the wonder of . . .

the colours in this peacock feather;

the pattern on this snail shell;

the carving my grandad did
. . . Amen.

A miracle tray

This is a picture of Thomas and Jane's miracle tray.
What have they put on it?
Have you got any of these things on *your* miracle tray?

PRAYER FOCUS 22

A miracle day

Explain to the children that today we are going to be on the look out for miracles. Talk together about all the miracles you notice:

– margarine melting when it is warm
– jelly setting in the fridge
– bubbles in the washing up water
– the way that television brings
   pictures from all over the world

If possible let the children experience an 'everyday miracle', e.g. by showing how an ice cube can melt to become water and water change to become steam.

What do they think are miracles?

At the end of the time remember all the miracles they have noticed and give thanks for them.

Ending Prayer

God, we worship you for the miracle and
   wonder of all we have seen today.
Help us to be observant and to notice all
   around us.
Help us to be quick to listen and to see all
   that is of wonder.
Help us to be alert to spot your miracles all
   around us. Amen.

A miracle day

Look at these pictures.
Do you think they show miracles?
Draw your own picture of a miracle in the space.

Fifth Prayer Mood
THINKING OF OTHERS

Do not worry about anything, but in everything by prayer and supplication with thanksgiving let your requests be made known to God. Philippians 4:6

This prayer mood is to introduce children to the idea of intercessory prayer. The Prayer Focuses are designed to encourage children towards an attitude of trust and faith and 'to be anxious for nothing'. However, *this* 'prayer mood' is *also* intended to awaken the realisation that prayer often leads us to an understanding of our own responsibilities to those we pray for.

A thanksgiving and blessing board

Explain to the children that God wants to know about us and to hear when we are happy or sad.

Together, make a simple pin board and ask the children to collect photographs, postcards and pictures from magazines which are significant for them. Try to choose bright colours and things which can be easily recognised. As part of the regular prayer pattern, look at the pictures together, simply saying: 'God bless . . .' or 'Thank you for . . .'

At first the collection of pictures can be very simple: trees, animals, photographs of relatives.

As the children gain in confidence they can arrange the board for themselves and the range of items could include pictures of nurses, firemen or houses and factories.

The intercessions can develop with the children's growing awareness, e.g. a thanksgiving for food may extend into a prayer for those without food and then onto a more specific prayer for a named part of the world.

Ending Prayer

We give thanks that we can be sure that God rejoices when we are happy and shares times when we are sad or anxious.
Today we give thanks for . . . .
We ask God's blessing on . . . .

Amen.

A thanksgiving and blessing board

THANK YOU GOD

GOD BLESS

Colour these headings for your thanksgiving and blessing board.

The light of the world

Find a picture of a candle, or photocopy the candle on the Focus Page for each child to cut out and colour. Pin the candles on a pin board.

With the children talk about how there are many different kinds of lights.

Talk about how light can comfort, cheer, guide, warn or celebrate.

Talk about how Jesus is sometimes called 'The light of the world'.

When the children know of particular people in need or in trouble, encourage them to put their name or picture under the candle.

Ending Prayer

(During the prayer time, help the children to compose a prayer related to the names or pictures around the candles.)

May the light of Jesus comfort . . . in their sadness.

May the light of Jesus help . . . in their pain.

May the light of Jesus guide . . . on their journey.

May the light of Jesus be with the celebrations at . . . party.

The light of the world

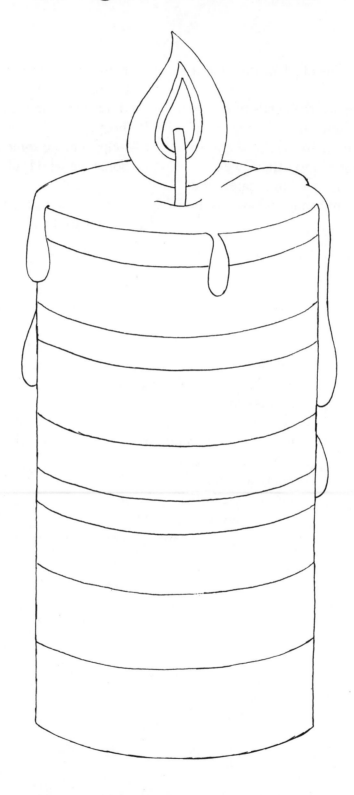

Here is a picture of a candle for you to colour and cut out for the Prayer Board.

PRAYER FOCUS 25

Christ has no hands but our hands

Draw a large outline of a hand and pin it on the board.

When praying for the needs of others help the children to consider what they can do to help. Help them to begin to understand that we are God's agents of love and care, and praying for people may involve us in action:

– could they ring Granny to cheer her up?
– draw a picture for their friend in hospital?
– help to make some shortbread for someone who is ill?

On the hand make a note of what they want to try to do.

Ending Prayer

Lord Jesus, when you lived on earth
  your hands brought comfort and healing
  to those in need.
Teach us to use our hands
  to serve those around us.
May we be willing to help,
  ready to work,
  imaginative in seeing the needs
  of those around us. Amen.

Christ has no hands but our hands

Are there ways you can be 'Jesus' hands' this week?
Draw or write what you plan to do on this hand.

Sixth Prayer Mood
TRUSTING

Behold I make all things new. Revelation 21:5

The focus of this prayer time is to develop the experience of trusting God and other people.

A resurrection walk

This focus is more easily undertaken in a rural setting, but in urban areas a park may provide enough stimulus.

Early in the year, take the children for a walk especially to look for signs of spring.

Invite them to use their eyes and ears to observe signs of new life: the building of nests, the sound of lambs, the opening buds of the hawthorn, the first celandines and snowdrops.

Talk about watching and waiting for new life to appear, after the bare trees and fields of winter.

Discuss the feelings of seeing the bare trees and watching for new life.

Talk about God's faithfulness in providing day and night and the seasons. We can trust in the power of God.

The children may like to learn this song to sing as they walk. The words fit the tune of 'Bobby Shaftoe' (see Appendix B):

Let's all search for signs of spring,
buds that burst and birds that sing,
listen to the bluebells ring
with the joy of springtime!

Chorus:
Life is bursting from the ground,
hope is dancing all around,
God, in ev'ry sight and sound
speaks of resurrection!

Though the ground is hard and cold,
watch the signs of life unfold,
God's amazing story told
in the joy of springtime!

Ending Prayer

We give thanks for the spring:
for the signs of new life,
for the light of longer days,
for the warmth of the sun,
for the opening of leaves and flowers,
for the song of the birds
and the beauty of newly born creatures.
We give thanks for a loving Creator
who makes all things new.

Amen.

A resurrection walk

**What can you see in this picture?
Is there anything there which you saw on your
resurrection walk?**

A trusting song

Teach the children the actions and chorus of the hymn 'God has promised' (*Come and Praise*, BBC Publucation).

Can you be sure that the rain will fall?
Make actions with hands to show rain falling.
Can you be sure that birds will fly?
Make actions with arms for flight of a bird.
Can you be sure that rivers will flow?
Make flowing wave movement with hands.
Or that the sun will light the sky?
Point to the sun in the sky.

Chorus:
God had promised.
God never breaks a promise he makes.
His word is always true.

Hold hands in a circle each time the chorus is sung.

Can you be sure that the tide will turn?
Turn to face outwards and then inwards.

Can you be sure that the grass will grow?
Make movement from ground upwards to represent grass growing.
Can you be sure that night will come?
Cover eyes with hands to show darkness of night.
Or that the sun will melt the snow?
Lift arms from waist upwards to show snow evaporating in the warmth.

You can be sure that God is near.
You can be sure he won't let you down.
You can be sure he'll always hear.
And that he's given Jesus, his Son.

For the last verse, walk in a circle clapping hands.

Talk about the words of the song. Ask the children if there are times when they feel that God is near. Are there special or everyday events when God seems very present to them? Remind them of Jesus' promise to be with us to the end of time.

Ending Prayer

Thank you, God, that you have promised to be near us always. Amen.

A trusting song

This is the first verse of the song we have just sung:
   Can you be sure that the rain will fall?
   Can you be sure that birds will fly?
   Can you be sure that rivers will flow?
   Or that the sun will light the sky?

Look at this picture and colour in the river.
Then draw the sun and the birds in the sky.
Colour the rest of the picture, then add a cloud and
   some rain.

71

PRAYER FOCUS 28

A trusting game

This can only be played when a child is happy to have a blindfold on without being uncomfortable or alarmed.

With the children, prepare the room with 'streams', 'mountains', 'marshes', 'dragons' and other obstacles.

Explain that the children will work in pairs, taking it in turn to be the leader or be led. The person who is led wears a blindfold. The leader has to give the partner careful instructions so that she/he keeps safe. It is advisable for only one pair to be moving at any one time to ensure safety.

Give an example by leading a child yourself first. Lead the child by the hand, giving her instructions so that she knows when there is a step or a narrow opening etc.

Talk about what it feels like to lead or be led.

Point out that the one who is blindfolded has to trust the one who leads, but the leader also has to trust that the one who is blindfolded doesn't peep!

Talk about how God can always be trusted to lead us safely.

Ending Prayer

Thank you, God, that we can trust you
to lead us safely throughout our lives.
Help us to trust you when our path is plain
and when we cannot see the way clearly.
Amen.

A trusting game

Here is a mask to colour and cut out.
You could use it to play a 'trusting game'.

Seventh Prayer Mood
IMAGINING

Let the children come to me: Mark 10:14

The focus of this prayer mood is to help the children to enter imaginatively into the story and to contemplate how different people in the story might be feeling.

Jesus and the children

Read or tell in your own words the story in Mark 10:13-16.

Encourage the children to imagine themselves with their parent(s) living at the time of Jesus.

- What would they have heard about Jesus?
- Would they want to see him?
- Would they ask their parent to take them to see Jesus?
- Would their mother or father want to go?
- Might they have to travel a long way?
- Would there be a crowd around Jesus?
- Who would be nearest Jesus?
- How would they feel when the disciples scolded them?
- Why do they think that the disciples turned them away?
- How would they feel when they heard Jesus contradicting the disciples?
- What did Jesus say?
- What do they think that meant?
- How did they feel when Jesus put his hands around them and blessed them?
- What would they remember about the day long afterwards?

Use a similar format with the children imagining themselves as a parent, a disciple, or Jesus himself.

Other stories which might be helpful to use for imaginative contemplation are Luke 2:8-20; Luke 19:1-10; Mark 11:7-11a and many more.

Ending Prayer

We give thanks for the love God showed us
in the person of Jesus.
Help us to know God loves, as children,
just as we are.

Amen.

Jesus and the children

This is a picture of Jesus with some children.
Imagine you are there.
There is a space in which you can draw yourself.
When you have done that, colour the whole picture.

Silence and sound

A listening story for use with Prayer Focus 6 (see page 18)

Listen to this story carefully. When it is finished, see how much detail you can remember.

One morning Joanna woke up early. It was a Saturday. She went to the window and pulled the curtains. The sun was shining and on the lawn she saw a blackbird looking for worms for its breakfast. Mr. Sarson, the next door neighbour, was already busy weeding his garden.

Joanna got dressed. She put on her blue dungarees, her yellow blouse and her red jumper.

She ran downstairs. Mr. Carlton, Joanna's Dad, was feeding Saucy their black cat. Joanna poured some cornflakes into a bowl and added milk and sugar. She was excited. Dad had promised to take her to the adventure playground today and her friend Sam was coming too.

Joanna and Dad packed up some lunch to take with them. They made cheese and tomato sandwiches, ham and cucumber rolls, and added a packet of onion flavoured crisps, three apples, and three cartons of blackcurrant juice to the lunch bag.

There was a knock at the door. Sam's Mum had arrived with Sam. She hugged Sam good-bye and waved as she went down the path. She was taking Sam's bigger brother to a football match that afternoon.

Mr. Carlton locked the back door, checked that they had got everything they needed for the day and the three set off for the bus stop. It was only a short ride to the adventure playground. From the top of the bus they could see so much. They went past the market, where Joanna noticed the stalls of brightly coloured materials and the fruit and vegetables piled up high. They went past the swimming pool and noticed the big sign outside with blue and white painted waves. Then the bus turned a corner and there ahead of them was the adventure playground.

There was so much to choose from – a high slide, nets to climb, ladders to reach higher walkways, swings, a tree house, a bouncing castle, see-saws, a roundabout. Joanna and Sam looked around wondering which to choose first.

Some music

Jesus' hands are kind hands

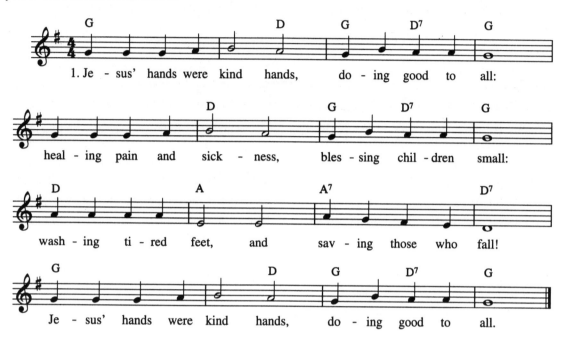

A rainbow song

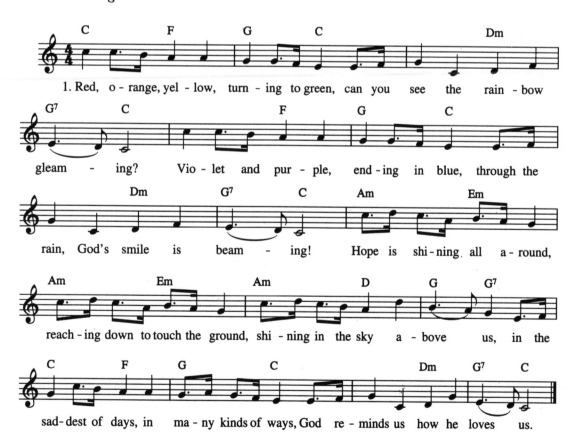

Signs of spring

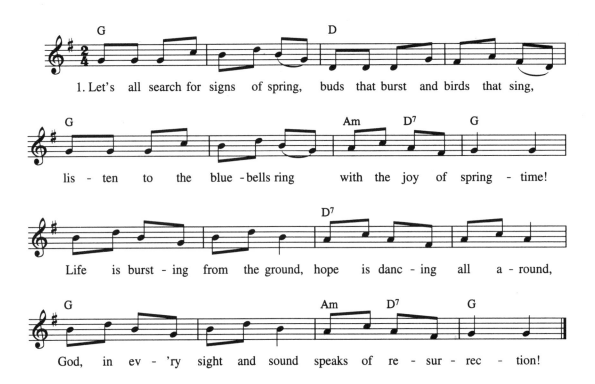

1. Let's all search for signs of spring, buds that burst and birds that sing,

lis - ten to the blue - bells ring with the joy of spring - time!

Life is burst - ing from the ground, hope is danc - ing all a - round,

God, in ev - 'ry sight and sound speaks of re - sur - rec - tion!